Caring for Your
Dog

Jill Foran

Weigl Publishers Inc.

Project Coordinator
Diana Marshall

Design and Layout
Warren Clark
Katherine Phillips

Copy Editor
Jennifer Nault

Photo Research
Gayle Murdoff

Locate the dog paw prints throughout the book to find useful tips on caring for your pet.

Published by Weigl Publishers Inc.
123 South Broad Street, Box 227
Mankato, MN 56002 USA
Web site: www.weigl.com

Library of Congress Cataloging-in-Publication Data

Foran, Jill.
  Caring for your dog / Jill Foran.
      v. cm. -- (Caring for your pet)
Contents: Man's best friend -- Doggy descriptions -- From the wild into the house -- A dog's life -- Picking your pup -- Dog supplies -- Dog diets -- Getting to know your dog -- Grooming your dog -- Dog duties -- Form packs to policing.
  ISBN 1-59036-033-8 (lib. bdg. : alk. paper)
 1. Dogs--Juvenile literature. [1. Dogs. 2. Pets.] I. Title. II. Caring for your pet (Mankato, Minn.)
  SF426.5 .F67 2002
  636.7--dc21

                        2002006117

Printed in the United States
2 3 4 5 6 7 8 9 0 06 05 04 03

Photograph Credits
Every reasonable effort has been made to trace ownership and to obtain permission to reprint copyright material. The publishers would be pleased to have any errors or omissions brought to their attention so that they may be corrected in subsequent printings.

Cover: dog in bathtub (Henryk Kaiser/MaXx Images Inc.); **Behling and Johnson Photography:** pages 10 top, 12, 18/19, 21 top, 21 bottom, 24, 25, 28; **Comstock Images:** pages 3, 4, 5 top left, 10 bottom, 11 bottom, 13, 14, 17 top, 20, 22, 30, 31; **Corel Corporation:** pages 8, 9 top, 9 bottom; **Lorraine Hill:** pages 15, 23; **Katherine Phillips:** page 11 top; **Photo Agora/Ken Schwab:** pages 6 left, 6 middle, 6 right, 7 left, 7 middle, 7 right; **PhotoDisc:** page 26 top; **Photofest:** page 27; **Picturesof.net:** title page, page 29; **Frances Purslow:** pages 6 right, 16; **Linda Weigl:** pages 5 bottom right, 17 bottom; **Bob Winsett/MaXx Images Inc.:** page 26 bottom left.

Contents

Puppy Pals

Dogs have been loyal companions to humans for thousands of years. All over the world, people keep dogs as pets because these animals are intelligent, loving, and faithful. They can bring us comfort when we are sad or lonely. Some dog **breeds** can also be trained to perform special jobs such as guiding, herding, or even policing.

Whenever your dog does something good, be sure to praise him in a warm, friendly voice.

Dogs make great pets because they are playful and energetic.

Fascinating Facts

- In 1957, a dog named Laika became the first creature to orbit Earth in a satellite.
- About one out of every three households in the United States has a dog.

Although dogs are great pets, looking after them takes time and patience. A dog must be fed, groomed, and exercised on a regular basis. The loyalty and affection that your dog gives you in return will make caring for him worth the effort.

Dogs are members of the *Canidae* family. They are related to wolves, coyotes, and foxes. While there is only one **species** of **domestic** dog, there are hundreds of different breeds. No other pet comes in such a large variety of shapes, sizes, and colors.

■ Dogs require plenty of love and attention.

■ Dogs can make us smile and laugh.

Pet Profiles

There are more than 400 breeds of dogs around the world. There are even more mixed breeds. Mixed-breed dogs, also called mutts, have parents that are of different breeds. All dogs, whether they are mutts or **purebreds**, have certain features and characteristics.

CHIHUAHUA

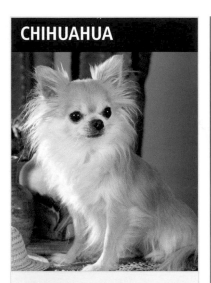

- Member of the **toy group**
- Smallest breed of dog
- Curious and alert
- Smooth, long **coat**
- Dome-shaped skull
- Fragile; does not like cold weather
- Can be aggressive; known to pick fights with larger dogs

SHAR-PEI

- Member of the **non-sporting group**
- Large head and wrinkled skin
- Rough coat
- One of oldest recognized breeds, dating back more than 2,200 years
- Was once used in China as a fighting dog
- Prefers the company of humans over dogs

BASENJI

- Member of the **hound group**
- Does not bark at all
- Coat is short and smooth
- **Tricolor,** chestnut red, or black in color
- Very affectionate and patient
- Independent
- Once used in Africa for hunting

In North America, dog breeds are divided into seven different groups. They are hound dogs, working dogs, sporting dogs, herding dogs, terrier dogs, toy dogs, and non-sporting dogs. Dog breeds are grouped according to their features, roles, and behavior. Knowing the breed and group features will help you pick the right type of dog for you and your family.

SIBERIAN HUSKY

- Member of the **working group**
- Eyes can be blue, brown, or sometimes one of each color
- Require plenty of exercise
- Friendly and gentle
- In cold climates, is used to pull sleds

BORDER COLLIE

- Member of the **herding group**
- Considered the world's best sheep-herding dog
- Usually black with white markings
- Energetic and intelligent
- Deep desire to please his owner

GOLDEN RETRIEVER

- Member of the **sporting group**
- One of the most popular household dogs
- Respected for his tracking abilities
- Friendly, eager to please, and very patient
- Coat is dense and water-repellent

Life Cycle

It is important for animal owners to learn about every stage of their pet's development. Over the years, your dog may have different requirements. At every stage of your dog's life, she needs love and attention.

Newborn Puppy

Puppies are born almost totally helpless. They cannot see, hear, or walk. Newborn puppies spend most of their time sleeping and drinking their mother's milk. It is very important to keep newborn puppies warm.

Adult Dog

If you take care of your dog, she will likely be healthy for many years. Still, older dogs slow down, and many begin to lose their hearing and eyesight. If this happens, your dog will need extra care and attention.

Fascinating Facts

- The average life span of a dog is 10 to 15 years.
- Three to six puppies make up an average litter.
- The oldest known dog was an Australian cattle-dog named Bluey. He lived for 29 years and 5 months.

Three to Nine Weeks

By about 3 weeks of age, puppies can see, hear, and walk. At 4 weeks, puppies begin to explore. Once their teeth begin to grow, puppies are ready to be **weaned**. This usually happens between 4 and 7 weeks. By the time they are 9 weeks old, they are ready to eat puppy food. A puppy should not be taken away from her mother and littermates until she is at least 8 weeks old.

One Year

After 1 year, most puppies have grown as big as they will grow. Some dogs may continue to gain weight until 2 years of age. They have learned a great deal by their first birthday, and their mental skills are fully developed. Dogs at this age need plenty of exercise and playtime.

Picking Your Pet

There are many things to consider before selecting a new dog. All dogs take a great deal of commitment. However, some breeds may fit into your lifestyle better than others. There are some important questions to think about before choosing your dog.

Before getting a dog, make sure no one in your household has pet allergies. Terriers and poodles are good choices for people with allergies.

What Do I Have Time For?

Do you have time to spend with an active puppy? Or would you prefer owning a more independent, adult dog? All dogs need attention, but puppies require the most time and effort. Be sure to choose a dog that you will have time to care for properly. Long-haired breeds take extra time because they need to be groomed at least once a day. Other breeds may require extra time for training.

There are many shelter dogs waiting to be adopted for a small fee.

How Big Will the Dog Become?

It is important to choose a dog whose size and shape suits your home. When selecting a dog, you should consider your living space. Is the size of your house or apartment better suited to a small dog or a large one? Getting a large dog is only an option if you have a big backyard where he can run and play.

■ Dogs need care and companionship. Do you have enough time to spend with a new pet?

How Much Will My Dog Cost?

Dogs can be costly. Purebred dogs and dogs from pet stores often come with expensive price tags. Another, less expensive, option is to get your dog from a shelter. Before you become a dog owner, be sure to consider how much money you will have to spend on your pet in future years. **Veterinary** care, food, and supplies are ongoing costs.

Fascinating Facts

- The smallest dog in history was a Yorkshire terrier from England. At 2 years of age, the dog stood 2.5 inches tall and weighed only 4 ounces.
- Smaller dogs usually live longer than larger breeds.

Dog Supplies

Moving to a new home can be stressful for many animal, including a dog. To help your dog adjust to a new home, be sure to stock up on a few essential supplies in advance. Important supplies include food and water dishes, a dog collar, a leash, a brush, a bed, and some toys.

Make sure that the toys you buy for your dog are strong. Do not give your dog small toys that may be swallowed.

Dogs love to chew bones, and play with toys, such as Frisbees and rubber balls.

One of the most important items to have for your new dog is a bed. All dogs need their own place to rest that is in a quiet area. Pet supply stores sell many styles and sizes of dog beds. These include plastic beds and basket-style beds. Some dog owners use a large cardboard box lined with blankets.

Dog owners must own a leash. When outdoors, a dog on a leash will be safe from speeding cars and other dangers. Along with keeping your dog safe, a leash is a good training tool.

■ Your dog will be happy with just about any bed you choose, as long as it is warm and comfortable.

Fascinating Facts

- New dog owners can calm a nervous puppy by placing a covered hot-water bottle in her bed. This reminds the puppy of the warmth of her mother and littermates.

Dog Diets

In order for your dog to be healthy, she must be given food that provides the proper nutrients and vitamins. Pet supply stores and veterinary clinics carry many brands of dog food. Talk to your **veterinarian** to find out which brands are best for your pet. You can buy dry food in the form of kibble, or moist food in cans. There are also special foods on the market for puppies and for older dogs.

Be sure to clean up antifreeze spills. Antifreeze can poison your dog if it is licked off your driveway.

■ Growing or hungry dogs can finish a bowl of dog food in minutes.

Fascinating Facts

- Dog biscuits are great treats because they help keep your dog's teeth healthy.
- Americans spend more money on dog food every year than they spend on baby food.
- Chocolate is poisonous to dogs.

While plastic bowls can be colorful, it is not as easy for your dog to chew through stainless steel bowls.

Giving your dog the correct amount of food is important. Puppies up to the age of 3 months should eat at least three meals a day. As your puppy gets older, her stomach can handle more food at one time. You may feed an older puppy fewer, but larger, meals. Adult dogs should be fed once or twice a day, at the same time every day. Fresh water should be available at all times.

A young, growing puppy needs to eat often.

From Nose to Toes

Dogs come in many shapes and sizes. From the tiny Chihuahua to the enormous Irish wolfhound, the appearances of dogs can be quite varied. Despite these differences, all dogs share the same **ancestors**. Their common ancestry means that all dogs, along with wolves, share a number of the same physical features.

WEIMARANER

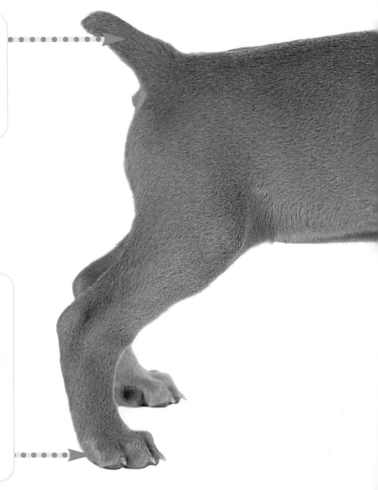

A dog often uses his tail to communicate his feelings. A wagging tail usually means a dog is happy, while a tail that is tucked in means he is afraid.

Dogs have long, slender feet. The heel of each foot is raised and does not touch the ground. This means that dogs always walk and run on their toes. Dogs also have tough pads at the bottom of each paw that absorb shock. Claws grip the ground as dogs walk.

Dogs have a very keen sense of hearing. Each ear has seventeen muscles. These muscles can raise, lower, and turn the outer ear flaps. A dog's ears are excellent sound receivers and locators.

Dogs do not see as well as humans. They have trouble seeing objects if they are too far away. They also see very little color. Dogs have a third eyelid that helps protect, cleanse, and moisten the eye.

Dogs rely on their sense of smell to identify all kinds of things. The bones inside the nose are covered with scent cells. This scent area is much larger than the scent area inside a human's nose. A dog's sense of smell is 1 million times better than a human's. A dog's nose also helps him control his body temperature.

Dogs use the whiskers on their chin, **muzzle**, and cheeks to touch and feel their surroundings. Their whiskers are connected to nerves, which make them very sensitive.

A dog has **incisors** that are used to scrape meat off bones. Behind the incisors are four long, sharp teeth called canine teeth. They are used for holding **prey**. Molars are wide, flat teeth at the back of the dog's mouth. They are used for grinding food.

Great Grooming

Your dog needs regular grooming to keep her looking and feeling her best. Regular brushing massages the dog's skin and promotes circulation. Grooming also removes dirt from your dog's coat and helps reduce **shedding**.

Different breeds of dogs need different kinds of grooming. Dogs with long hair need to be combed and brushed every day. Dogs with short hair need less attention. When grooming your dog, you should always brush her fur in the same direction that it grows. Once you have brushed the dog's back, hold her head up and brush down the throat and between the front legs. Carefully brush the fine hair on your dog's stomach with gentle strokes.

When bathing your dog, use a gentle shampoo that is made for puppies or dogs.

■ Frequent brushing keeps a dog's coat in good condition.

When bathing your dog, be sure to restrain her so that she does not struggle and hurt herself.

Grooming your dog is the best way to keep her clean. Most dogs do not need baths often. In fact, three or four baths a year is usually enough. Dogs that spend a great deal of time outdoors may need to be bathed about once a month.

Fascinating Facts

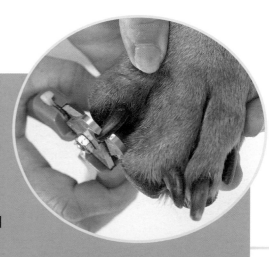

- Trimming your dog's toenails is an important grooming activity. Many foot disorders in dogs result from long toenails. Claw clipping can be tricky. Never attempt to clip your dog's claws until a veterinarian has first shown you how it is done.
- Early peoples in Mexico used the fur of long-haired Chihuahuas to make clothing.

Healthy and Happy

Dogs are generally healthy animals. There are some things you can do to help keep them in top condition. Proper feeding, grooming, and plenty of exercise are all important for maintaining a healthy dog. New dog owners should bring their pet to a veterinarian right away. The veterinarian may give your dog **vaccinations**, which help to prevent dog diseases. Puppies should receive their first vaccinations when they are about 6 to 8 weeks old. After that, the veterinarian will give your dog shots only when they are needed.

Inspect your dog every day to make sure he does not have split toenails, tics, or fleas.

■ Take your dog to the veterinarian at least once a year. Regular checkups will help keep your pet healthy.

Dogs have ways of letting you know when they are sick. Changes in behavior, loss of appetite, diarrhea, and a dull coat are all signs that something is wrong. As soon as you notice any of these kinds of changes in your pet, take him to see a veterinarian.

Exercising your dog every day will keep him in good shape and help him maintain a proper weight. Exercise also decreases your dog's risk of getting heart disease.

■ Walking your dog is an important part of keeping her fit. When she is exercising in public, your dog must wear a collar and tag.

Fascinating Facts

- In most countries, the law states that your dog must have vaccinations every year to protect against **rabies** and other dog diseases.

Dog Duties

Dogs are social animals. Long ago, when they lived in the wild, they were part of groups called packs. Each dog pack had a leader that made the rules and watched over the others. Today, most dogs think of their human family as their pack. This means that your new dog will expect you, or someone in your household, to be the leader. If no one in your home acts like the leader, your dog will become confused. He may even try to become the leader himself.

By teaching your dog obedience, you can show him that you are in charge.

Pet Peeves

Dogs do not like:
- nervous strangers
- people in uniforms
- people with umbrellas
- having their feet touched
- being left in a hot car
- being left home alone all day
- not having water in their bowl when they need a drink

It is best to begin training your dog when he is a puppy. Puppies are eager to please and easily trained. If you need help training your dog, enroll in obedience school. You can also read books about dog obedience.

Dogs need to learn how to behave properly around other animals, especially other dogs. Allowing your pet to meet new dogs will make him more comfortable around them. This will also make him a better walking companion.

■ Training takes time and practice, but it is worth it in the end. Some owners enter their pets into obedience competitions at dog shows.

Fascinating Facts

- Some dogs bark more than others. The world record for constant barking is held by a cocker spaniel who barked 907 times in only 10 minutes.
- The basenji is the only breed of dog that cannot bark.

Role Call

Dogs have been taught to perform important jobs in society. Herding dogs are trained to help farmers look after livestock. Guard dogs are taught to protect homes and businesses from intruders. Seeing-eye dogs act as the eyes for people who are blind. They guide their owners safely along crowded sidewalks and lead them around obstacles. People should never distract a seeing-eye dog. He needs to pay attention to helping his owner at all times. Dogs can also be taught to help people who are in wheelchairs.

■ Police and fire dogs are trained to protect people and to find illegal items, such as explosives.

■ Rescue dogs can sniff out survivors after earthquakes and avalanches. Others can locate drowning victims.

Fascinating Facts

- Newfoundland dogs are used as lifeguards on some beaches in France.

In 1954, Lassie made her television debut. The show took place on an American family farm.

The very first movie to star a dog was called *Rescued by Rover*. It was made in England in 1905. Since then, a wide variety of dogs have appeared in films, television shows, commercials, and books.

The book *Lassie Come Home* was written in 1940. The story is about a collie named Lassie. Lassie lives in Yorkshire, England. The dog's owners must sell her because they need money. Lassie's new owners take her to Scotland. The adventures begin when Lassie attempts to make the long journey home. This story inspired a television series and a movie.

Long Lost Friend

The tale of Argus in *The Odyssey* is about a dog's devotion to his master. When the young Greek king, Odysseus, goes to war against the Trojans, he leaves his family behind. He also leaves his faithful dog, Argus. It is 20 years before Odysseus returns. He comes back disguised as a beggar. Walking to his home, Odysseus meets Argus lying on the ground. The dog has aged and is close to death. Still, Argus recognizes his master through the disguise. The weak dog lifts his head and struggles to rise to greet Odysseus. Argus receives a loving hug from his master and is finally able to die in peace.

Taken from Homer's *The Odyssey*.

Pet Puzzlers

What do you know about dogs? If you can answer the following questions correctly, you may be ready to own a pet dog.

Q What kinds of animals are dogs' closest relatives?

Dogs are members of the *Canidae* family. Their closest relatives are wolves, coyotes, and foxes.

Q Why is obedience training important for a pet dog?

Since dogs are such social animals, it is important for their owners to lead them. In the wild, dogs lived in packs that had a leader. Owners must lead their dogs by setting the rules and regulations of the household.

Q When are puppies ready to be weaned?

Normally, puppies are ready to be weaned when they are between 4 and 7 weeks old.

Q Why is it important to buy a bed for your dog?

A pet dog needs a soft and comfortable place to sleep when she is tired. She also needs a place of her own for peace and quiet.

Q How often should dogs be exercised?

Most dogs should be exercised every day. Daily walks will keep a pet dog healthy and at a proper weight. Exercise also decreases a dog's risk of heart disease.

Q When are dogs thought to have become domesticated by humans?

Experts believe that dogs were domesticated more than 10,000 years ago.

Dog Tags

Before you buy your pet dog, write down some dog names that you like. Some names may work better for a female dog. Others may suit a male dog. Here are just a few suggestions:

Benji

Spot

Rover

Jake

Sam

Max

Charlie

Molly

Lucy

Bear

Frequently Asked Questions

Why should I have my dog spayed or neutered?

Spaying (for female dogs) and neutering (for male dogs) are medical operations that make it impossible for dogs to produce puppies. Every year, millions of unwanted puppies are born because dog owners did not get their dogs spayed or neutered. Most of these puppies go to shelters because there are not enough homes for them. As a responsible pet owner, you should have your dog spayed or neutered. This will help prevent the births of too many dogs. Also, spaying or neutering your dog can improve your pet's health.

Is it safe to give my dog a bone?

While chewing bones can help keep a dog's mouth healthy, many veterinarians believe that bones are a big risk. Some bones are so hard that they can chip your dog's teeth. It is even more dangerous to give your dog chicken or lamb bones. These bones can splinter, and damage a dog's throat and stomach. Find something that is safer for your dog to chew.

Why does my dog walk in circles before she lies down?

It is natural for your dog to walk in circles before lying down. Dogs in the wild have done this for thousands of years. They are simply rearranging their bed to make sure that it is comfortable and to make sure the area is safe.

More Information

Animal Organizations

You can help dogs stay happy and healthy by learning more about them. Many organizations are dedicated to teaching people how to care for and protect their pet pals. For more dog information, write to the following organizations:

American Dog Owners Association
1654 Columbia Turnpike
Castleton, NY 12033

Humane Society of the United States
2100 L Street N.W.
Washington, DC 20037

Web Sites

To answer more of your dog questions, go online and surf to the following Web sites:

American Kennel Club
www.akc.org

Care for Animals
www.avma.org/careforanimals/
animatedjourneys/animatedfl.asp

Pet Place
www.petplace.com

Words to Know

ancestors: early animals from which later species developed

breeds: groups of animals that share specific characteristics

coat: a dog's fur

descended: to come from the same family line

domestic: tame and used to living among people; not wild

evolved: to develop gradually

herding group: breeds used to control the movement of other animals

hound group: breeds that search for hunted animals by smell and sight

incisors: front teeth used for cutting, tearing, or chewing

muzzle: the part of an animal's face that juts out and includes the jaw, mouth, and nose

non-sporting group: breeds of sturdy dogs that include a variety of types

prey: animals that are hunted and killed by other animals for food

purebreds: animals whose relatives are known and in whom the same traits have been passed down through generations

rabies: a disease that can cause death

shedding: losing fur

species: a group of organisms that shares biological features

sporting group: breeds noted for being active and alert; good in the water

toy group: breeds noted for their small size

tricolor: having three colors

vaccinations: injections of medicines that help prevent certain diseases

veterinarian: animal doctor

veterinary: medical treatment of animals

weaned: stopped drinking a mother's milk

working group: breeds noted for their large size and strength

Index